The

Guide

to

Fabulous Fowey

Phil Billington

ISBN 09553648 5 X
ISBN 978-09553648-5-3

Published by
Polperro Heritage Press
Clifton-upon-Teme
Worcestershire WR6 6EN UK
www.polperropress.co.uk

Printed by Orphans Press
Leominster HR6 0LD
United Kingdom

Contents

INTRODUCTION

Within these pages I have tried to capture the many facets that make Fowey what it is today. It cannot be adequately described in words, nor portrayed by photographs. Fowey speaks for itself. Its outstanding beauty and character will not fail to enchant anyone who experiences it. Those who visit are honoured and upon leaving cannot wait to return.

This guide has been designed to not only be read from cover to cover, but also to be dipped into at will. The photographs speak volumes and aid the reader to identify where they are, even if they don't know!

It seems rather fitting really, that to pronounce Fowey, one only needs to remember that it was once spelt 'Foy' and that it rhymes with both joy and enjoy.

So enjoy the joy of 'Fabulous Fowey'.

Phil Billington 2008

FOWEY

There's so much more to Fowey than just pasties, ice cream or being by the seaside. It's historic, quaint, beautiful and most desirable. It has style, natural grace and is totally and utterly stunning. Its streets may be narrow and parking difficult, but oh what a joy to behold. Unique, breathtaking, wonderful and with the added bonus, it's on the Cornish coast.

The harbour is natural, spacious and glorious. The views are fantastic, equal to any, if not superior, and the whole place is overflowing with character and characters. Mere descriptions cannot do Fowey the full justice it deserves. Its beauty does not ebb and flow like the ceaseless tide that visits. Once seen, it will haunt the memory until one's return.

This part of the coastline has been deservedly designated an area of outstanding beauty and much is protected by the National Trust. So, not only is Fowey an estate agents' dream, but a tourist one too. Those lucky Cornish Piskies have indeed worked overtime here.

The Cornish for Cornwall is 'Kernow' and the town's Cornish name seems to have been derived from 'fou' meaning 'beech river'. It is still heavily wooded and this only enhances its charm, especially during autumn when the colours and reflections are magnificent. Its name has been variously spelt such ways as 'Fawi', 'Fauwy', 'Foy' and 'Foye'. A rose by any other name…

The town is restricted by the river and also by the boundaries of Place, the ancient ancestral home of the Treffry family. Most of central Fowey is situated on the level, but there are some steep areas as well.

Fowey has obvious sea connections and has thus been a centre for fishing, shipbuilding, sailing, trading and alike for centuries past. But the glory days of pilchards, tin, and copper are long gone and the main industry now seems to be tourism, which is thriving. Cornwall in general and Fowey in particular, make a dream holiday come true. Just look at the joy in the faces of the visitors.

From the headland, beach and buildings at Readymoney Cove, down through the centre of town and along to Caffa Mill by the Bodinnick car ferry crossing, Fowey is just a total delight.

TOWN QUAY

The Town Quay lies at the very heart of Fowey and is an absolute must to visit. A camera and perhaps a good pair of binoculars are essential here, as the panoramic views are just glorious. This area and parts of nearby streets are liable to very occasional high spring tide flooding. There have been times when people have proceeded along the high street in a rowing boat!

Just soak up the bustling atmosphere for a while. Watch youngsters enthusiastically crabbing. If the tide is out, there is a small exposed beach to walk on. Look out over to the open sea, towards St. Catherine's and St. Saviour's headlands and to the ancient Blockhouse.

Gaze over to Polruan with its shipbuilding yards, to the inlet of Pont Pill and the tree-lined route of the Hall Walk, or over to Prime Cellars, Ferryside and beyond to the car ferry at Bodinnick. Watch the china clay ships arrive and depart, the Polruan passenger ferry plying to and fro along with all the other vessels on the water and you will not be bored. Enjoy this panoramic harbour scene; it's Fowey at its very best.

Looking towards the buildings of the town quay, part of the Galleon public house can be seen and the beautiful mellow coloured brickwork of the Working Men's Institute. High above are the crenulated walls and towers of Place, which look rather like a castle.

A flight of steps lead up to the King of Prussia public house, with its impressive display of hanging baskets and window boxes. Behind is the tall, solid tower of the church. The inviting signs of the aquarium and a couple of restaurants with a fast food outlet in-between complete the scene. The local seagulls are also rather partial to a 'take-away', so be on guard; it's like *The Birds* all over again! Not just content with that, they treat bin bags as personally wrapped snacks. So much so in fact, that when locals put rubbish out on the mornings of collection, they protect the bags from attack by covering them with blankets and sheets. There is even now a specially designed 'gull guard' sheet for sale! It's the cosiest rubbish in the Duchy! Many of the litterbins bear the message 'please do not feed the seagulls'. Jackdaws also seem to be muscling in on this banquet now and some ducks have even resorted to begging! You have been warned!

The ferry over to Polruan regularly departs from the Town Quay and is an excellent way to view the harbour and its various landmarks. Note however that during the summer months it departs from Whitehouse Slip in the day and from the Town Quay early evening onwards till late. The service is frequent and inexpensive. There is also a water-taxi available, which takes moored visitors from ship to shore.

Self-drive hire boats are great fun and other trips are available and can be booked here in advance. These include sea cruises to places like Polperro, Mevagissey, Charlestown, Polkerris and Lantic Bay. There are also regular river trips upstream to Golant, Lerryn and even Lostwithiel, the old medieval capital of Cornwall. Guided harbour tours, one even in a small steam launch, are a great way of seeing the sights. These journeys are dependent upon tide, weather and water conditions, but if all are suitable, this is an excellent and thoroughly absorbing way to spend some quality time. For an interesting town tour, take the yellow 'train' ride.

WORKING MEN'S INSTITUTE

This elegant building was erected in 1868 and was built on the former site of an old fish market and a public house. The Royal British Legion is now housed here. Bar and hot drinks facilities are open to the public.

Outside, Service Boards once displayed listings of lifeboat rescues. These noted the nature of the rescue, the name of the vessel involved and the number of lives saved or lost. They made poignant reading and are now housed within the R.N.L.I. premises, the shop being located in Passage Street.

KING OF PRUSSIA

This ever-popular pub, rebuilt in 1886, has a similar design to an even earlier one bearing the same name. Beneath it can be seen the granite pillars of an old market.

The name is derived either from John Carter, a Cornish smuggler whose nickname was the 'King of Prussia', or Frederick the Great, one time King of Prussia. Look out for the sign outside; unusually it has different pictures on both sides. Perhaps the artist couldn't decide on the origins of the name either!

Like many of the local public houses this one is owned and supplied by the St. Austell Brewery Company, independent family brewers of St. Austell and founded by William Hicks in 1851. Be sure to look out for Duchy bitter, Black Prince, Tinners, H.S.D. (Hicks Special Draft) and the ever-popular Tribute ale.

AQUARIUM

The building was originally part of an old market and was converted in 1950. It exhibits weird and wonderful local marine specimens, is cool relief from the summer's heat and has a children's 'touch' pool. Here they can be in contact with the strange, fascinating creatures of the deep. A must for all. Open May to September. An admission fee is charged.

FOWEY MUSEUM

Just round the corner to the left of the aquarium is this rather compact local museum. Many interesting artefacts such as General Garibaldi's cloak, which was worn on his visit of 1864, are on display. The museum is well worth a look inside, as it contains a fascinating insight into the long history of Fowey and its inhabitants. Open May to September. An admission fee is charged.

TOWN HALL

The Town Hall was built in 1793 and contains the museum and former council chambers. Part can be seen between the museum and the aquarium, but is sadly not always open to the public. It retains some of the previous medieval features of the 14th century guild chapel building it replaced, such as the iron barred windows of the old jail.

At the back of the building by the public telephone box and toilets, can be seen the site of the old town water tap, installed in 1787, to the then great delight of all. Nowadays, clean, fresh water is a commodity taken for granted, but back then it was a luxury and rather special. Ironically the tap no longer works although its modern chrome replacement does.

ST. FIMBARRUS' CHURCH

This charming, historic church is dedicated to the Irish missionary St. Finn Barr and the substantial four staged tower, built in the 1460s, is the second highest in Cornwall, Probus near Truro being the first.

The present church has a 12th century carved but unfinished font. The pulpit was constructed in 1601 from the panels of a Spanish Galleons captain's room. A rather uncommon priest's chamber is present, being a special room above the main entrance. Also to be seen is a splendid 15th century wagon roof, an interesting bell-ringers' board, fascinating monuments, ancient brasses, 'Q's special pew and many other features of merit.

Reasonably priced guidebooks are available for purchase inside the church and visitors are most welcome. For details of services see outside board to the left of the main entrance gates.

The bell ringers practise on a Friday evening and this is a joy to hear. It feels as if the sound of history itself is being summoned, as though the past is brought into the present. From the warning of various enemy attacks down throughout the centuries, the mournful plague bells of 1625 when many a local was a tragic victim, through to the rejoicing peals for weddings, christenings, coronations, jubilees, calling of the faithful and for countless other reasons, the bells have been witness.

It was in this church, in 1899, that Kenneth Grahame was married. Author Sir Arthur Quiller-Couch, often known by the pseudonym 'Q', was himself Grahame's witness. The pageboy was Sir Arthur's eight-year-old, only son, Bevil Quiller-Couch, who was later to sadly die in the army in 1919, aged 29.

The war memorial in the churchyard is a thought-provoking reminder of those who gave their lives and bears Bevil's name. A rather touching result of all this was that Bevil's horse 'Peggy' was later returned to Fowey by the army and looked after by the family. Even more ironic, is the fact that the war memorial was erected on the site of an old public house called the Rose and Crown, the landlord of which, in 1812, was hung for a local murder.

To the side of the church, a short, steep footpath with plenty of benches leads up through the small closed cemetery to some interesting old almshouses to the right at Cobb's Well. Some date back to before the 1630s. The tall walls of Place and glimpses of the building can be seen.

Continuing up the hill, one arrives at the Safe Harbour public house. Opposite is Hanson Drive, which has excellent harbour views. Named after Sir Charles Hanson, for whom Fowey Hall was constructed along here in 1899, it is now a hotel and host to the Daphne du Maurier Festival of Arts and Literature held every year.

At the start of the drive to the left is a small memorial garden called the Piggy Lane Triangle. This is just delightful and has an old signpost, a board explaining the panoramic view and glorious planting. Behind the Central Car Park to the left of a few grey houses can be found the remains of the old tower windmill.

PLACE

Since the 1300s, this fortified manor house has been the private stronghold of the important and influential Treffry family. It was built in 1260. The name means 'house' in Cornish.

Around 1457, the flames of the French attack burned high over Fowey. Fire destroyed most of the buildings as Elizabeth Treffry of Place heroically defended her home. With the help of her loyal men she bravely ousted the enemy. Place was rebuilt and has been much added to over the years. Splendid monuments to the family can be seen in the nearby church of St. Fimbarrus.

Place commands a dominant position above Fowey and can often be mistaken for part of the church. Due to its high location within the town, it is best viewed from the water. Today it is still in Treffry family ownership and although a private residence, the grounds can be used for weddings. It has been occasionally open to the public for garden fetes. Strawberries and cream on the 'lawns of history'. If only walls could talk, what fantastic stories this 'place' could tell.

SHOPS & SERVICES

There is a wide variety of shops and services available in these narrow streets. Thankfully mostly situated in the flattest part of Fowey. There is a wealth of restaurants, café's and assorted eating-places, many of which specialise naturally enough in seafood dishes. It is well worthwhile taking full advantage of this fact as locally caught produce is both delicious and fresh.

The world famous Cornish pasty has its origins in the mining industry. Being stuck underground on a long shift, Cornishmen needed a substantial meal, hence the pasty was born. Its traditional thick 'crimped' edge was the 'holding handle', being thrown away afterwards by the dirty-handed miner. The filling was a matter of taste but usually involved steak, potato, onion and turnip or swede in varying proportions depending on where in Cornwall it was made. Strangely enough fish is not a common ingredient. Often one corner of the pasty contained a pudding filling. Frequently the owner had his name, initials or some sort of symbol on the baked pastry, for ease of identification.

So there it is, an all in one, disposable and fully biodegradable main meal with dessert included, being delicious, substantial and nutritious. Some miners would often leave a small piece of pasty to appease the spirits of the mine, namely the 'knockers'. Not doing so could well result in their displeasure leading to such bad luck as falling stones, barren seams or worse. Sadly the mines are all but a relic of the past now but the pasty lives on forever. Every year a giant pasty is baked at Polruan for the Fowey Regatta and ferried over with great celebration. Pasties are often referred to by the nickname 'oggies'.

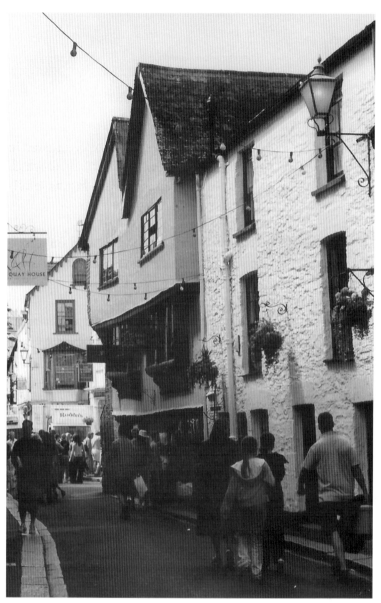

So from food to fashion, souvenirs, objets d'art, pottery, antiques, sailmakers, marine chandlers, banks, a large variety of accommodation and so much more besides, Fowey has it all. It can even boast a butcher, a baker and yes, a candlestick maker! Polruan has only a few shops remaining, when once it boasted many.

For tourist information, the Tourist Board is situated within the Ticket & du Maurier Literary Centre in South Street next to the main church behind the town quay. The staff are most helpful and can even arrange talks and sightseeing tours around Fowey. These are usually bookable in advance and cost is nominal.

Along the streets can be found many charming and interesting buildings. Noah's Ark and Well House are both of special merit. Noah's Ark is a timbered Elizabethan merchants house, dating back to the early 15th century, surviving the French attack and burning of the town in 1456. The ground floor now houses a dental surgery. Next door is Well House, formally known as The Old House of Foye, built in 1430. Inside is an original fireplace with some of the old cobbled floor exposed. The well can be visited. In the recent past this building was a folk museum and home to artist Billie Graeme.

Apart from the King of Prussia, there are a number of other public houses, such as the Lugger that was built in 1633 and the Galleon. Both are in Fore Street, although the Galleon also has an entrance on the town quay. In Lostwithiel Street can be found the Ship Inn, which was established in 1570, being a former Elizabethan town house of the influential and important Rashleigh family. Further up the hill in Lostwithiel Street is the Safe Harbour, which was built in the early 1800s and was formally known as the 'Commercial Inn'. All are of great character, rich in history and worth further investigation! For a week in May some are host to the lively Fowey Fringe Folk Festival.

It is very hard to imagine that before the early 1960s, there was two-way traffic through Fowey. Thankfully a one-way system is in place now and through traffic is kept to a minimum with the aid of nearby car parks. It is only a short walk then into the centre of town and a park and ride service is available.

The narrow old streets of Fowey were never built to accommodate the modern motorcar and in places the numerous scratches on the walls bear testament to this. Even now there is talk of banning cars altogether. Pity the poor old horses and ponies of days long gone pulling laden carts and traps here, as the streets were never built with their comfort in mind either.

AROUND & ABOUT FOWEY HARBOUR

Fantastic views of the river and harbour can be seen from many vantage points. The most spectacular ones being from above Readymoney Cove at St. Catherine's Point in Fowey, from the headland of St. Saviour's Point above Polruan and from the Hall Walk, which stretches from Bodinnick round to Polruan. All are breathtaking and well worth the effort. At night the harbour is illuminated by a myriad of lights and looks stunning. Both the Blockhouse and St. Catherine's Castle are floodlit, creating an atmospheric focus.

The River Fowey, having its source high up on Bodmin Moor, lies at the very heart of Fowey. It has been most appropriately described as the 'main road' in and out of town, being the port of destination or departure for many a 'salty dog'. The sea has been the life-blood of the area for many centuries and the waters are as busy today as ever. From shipbuilding traditions and sailing in general, to sailors on the seven seas, trading and smuggling, privateering and wars, the bravado of the Fowey Gallants of old, the catching, pressing and salting of fish, to the Royal Fowey Yacht Club and other such traditions, Fowey and the sea have been inextricably linked together

down throughout time. Fowey has sailing roots second to none and it is not uncommon for tall ships to visit, helping to reinforce this link with the past. Just listen to the sound of the wind in the rigging of the countless vessels in the harbour nowadays; it's an echo from yesteryear.

The title 'Fowey Gallants' the name now given to a sailing club, was originally given to the seamen of Fowey for their great audacity at the battles of Crecy and Calais in 1346 when the English defeated the French. The Royal Fowey Yacht Club was founded in 1894 and was formally the Yacht Club, established in 1880. The excellent Fowey Royal Regatta and Carnival Week takes place every summer in August and a host of events attract many a visitor and competitor alike. To the delight of all, the Red Arrows display team are a regular annual feature.

A large variety of shipping visits annually, with passenger liners and china clay boats making full use of the deep waters. Trips upstream, hire boats and even ferries give the visitor a taste aboard and are an excellent way to view the area.

When out in a hire-boat remember always to put safety first and give others plenty of room. When looking and travelling forward, port is on the left represented by a red light and starboard is on the right represented by a green light. So when giving way to other craft, one should do so by passing to the right of them on your starboard green side. They will then be on your left or port red side. They should do the same and so both craft will pass each other port-to-port. Watch the boats in the harbour to see if they do this. Power gives way to sail and everything gives way to the lifeboats, as they do to the clay boats. Very large vessels have restricted turning and so have priority.

It's fascinating to see the names of all the yachts and other craft and find out where they originate. Those bearing the letters FY are ones registered at Fowey. Many of the small flags flown have a specific meaning; such as when leaving port the signal flag 'Blue Peter' is traditionally flown, being blue with a central white square.

Cornwall has its own national emblem, a coat of arms that includes a sea fisherman, a tin miner and a bird, the Cornish chough. Within a shield depicting the waves of the sea are fifteen yellow circles on a black inner shield. These are thought to represent gold raised in the 9th century for the ransom payment of the captured Duke or Earl of Cornwall, who was held by the Saracens during the Crusades. The symbol is often to be seen around Fowey on street bollards. A scroll at the base of the coat of arms bears the county motto 'one and all' referring to the raising of that ransom by the generous Cornish.

All over Cornwall, on land as well as sea, can be found the flag of St. Piran being a white cross on a black background. This is said to represent either the triumph of good over evil or white tin deposits found in a black hearth or dark rock. St. Piran's Day is celebrated on March 5th and he is the patron saint of tinners. The flag has become a symbol of Cornish pride and independence, being proudly flown throughout the Duchy.

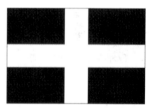

Sea mists and damp drizzly conditions often result in a weather condition called 'mizzle'. This is common in Cornwall and is guaranteed to soak through to the bone. Very occasionally, storms out to sea disturb a certain type of plankton in the bay that then drifts inshore. Its special properties produce after dark a luminescent effect, a phenomenon that can be spectacular when seen in the wake of a boat or if one tries skimming stones.

There have been several ships named 'Fowey' over the years. One HMS *Fowey,* a Royal Navel vessel, was constructed in 1749 but not locally. It saw valiant action in the Seven Years War and the American War of Independence before being sunk at Yorktown on the south-east American seaboard. Another vessel was the *Fowey* constructed in Hull in 1744. It worked in the Gulf of Mexico in 1748 and was captained, interestingly enough, by one 'Francis Drake', but obviously not the famous 16th century navigator and buccaneer. The *Francis of Foy* owned by John Rashleigh of Place was involved in 1588 with Sir Francis Drake's successful victory over the Spanish Armada. A mostly local crew manned the triumphant ship. Both Drake and Raleigh have visited and sailed from Fowey.

The busy harbour is a natural, sheltered, safe haven for all types of craft. James Cook, namesake of his famous father, surveyed it in 1786. Famous visitors have included author Daniel Defoe, poet Alfred Lord Tennyson, artists J.M.W. Turner and Joseph Southall, Queen Victoria and Prince Albert, the inventor Marconi, the Italian patriot Garibaldi, Queen Elizabeth II and Prince Phillip and even the famous tea clipper the *Cutty Sark* in 1924. Queen Elizabeth I was a guest at Place and her chair is said to be still preserved there. Charles I was nearly murdered here in 1644.

Another person worth mentioning is one who 'went away' rather than arrived. A local fisherman's daughter, Mary Broad, aged 21, was sentenced to hang in 1786 for committing highway robbery by stealing a cloak. Instead, luckily for Mary, she was sent for transportation to Botany Bay in Australia. She married another felon, one William Bryant and together they escaped in epic style. They were captured and the now Mary Bryant was once again in the shadow of the hangman's noose. She was finally pardoned in 1793 and free to return to Cornwall.

Fowey harbour and the surrounding area is an attractive place for all sorts of absorbing interests, sailing being most obvious. There are pontoons for visiting craft to use and these are situated between Penleath Point and

Prime Cellars and also in the entrance to Pont Pill. They are provided by the Harbour Commissioners and mooring charges apply. There are frequent sailing competitions and lessons available.

Two fully equipped lifeboats are on 24-hour standby, as are the coastguards and pilots helping to keep all safe and secure. The locally based lifeboat is the Trent Class *Maurice and Joyce Hardy* with a crew of six and can reach a speed of 25 knots. There is also the 'D' Class *Olive Herbert* inshore lifeboat available for service which crews three and can reach a speed of twenty knots. These mostly voluntary crews risk life and limb for the benefit of others. The warning maroons (two consecutive loud bangs) are only too frequently heard. It is to the great credit of all involved that within minutes of this they are out on the water and racing towards what is hopefully yet another successful rescue. Now deemed too 'noisy' by some, maroons are not always used.

There is a Royal National Lifeboat Institute shop in Passage Street and together with many other local shops; businesses and individuals raise valuable funds through various sales and charity events.

Both Fowey and Polruan were great fishing centres in the past, this being the mainstay of many a family. The pilchard was considered to be the king of fish and an old saying went thus: 'Pilchards are food, money and light and all in one night'. Around the harbour hung the rich smell of fish as the pilchards were pressed for their valuable oil and salted fresh from the nets. There are a few fishing boats that work out from Fowey these days, but they are just a mere shadow of the fleet and industry that once flourished here. How things have changed. The fishermen of old would turn in their graves if they only knew the present value of their humble cottages. It seems to be the trend now, that an ever-increasing amount of properties are second homes or holiday lets. Local, prospective house purchasers cannot always afford to buy, as the cost can often be way out of reach. Fowey may be an estate-agents' dream, but it can also be a local's nightmare, especially for first-time buyers.

Fishing as a hobby is very popular here, either by boat or from the shore and there is a local tackle shop near Caffa Mill Car Park. The inlets and especially the harbour and bay are excellent. Half or full day fishing trips can be booked by the town quay and there are even self-drive hire boats to rent out by the hour or longer if required. There are many opportunities for fishing around the harbour from rocks and beaches. Some of the most favoured places are off the rocks at St.Catherine's Point in Readymoney Cove, around the Whitehouse Slip area; from both sides of the Bodinnick ferry area (remembering to keep well away from the actual ferryboats), from the old ferry slipway point off Passage Street, Fowey and by the Blockhouse rocks in Polruan. There are many other places besides, but wherever one goes, safety is the key word. Beware of tides, falling and slippery rocks, watercraft and not putting one's self or others in any sort of dangerous place or position. If when fishing the only thing caught is sunburn, there is an excellent fishmonger in Fore Street to protect pride and a chemist to ease pain!

Swimming is not generally recommended because of the numerous yachts and various shipping in and around the harbour. It is fine, however, within the shelter of Readymoney Cove, where there is a purpose-built floating pontoon and the entrance is barred to boats. Beware of underwater rock ledges close to the cliffs. You may meet a dolphin!

Fowey is a great place for painting and affords many landscape and seascape opportunities. This idyllic setting has attracted the likes of J.M.W. Turner, who created the atmospheric watercolour entitled 'The Entrance to Fowey Harbour'. Other famous artists such as Rowlandson, Daniel and Southall have sketched and painted the fine views. There are a couple of galleries in central Fowey that sell original work.

This area is idyllic for bird watching and a great variety can be seen. Apart from the obligatory ducks and gulls, a probable tick list includes the: cormorant, puffin, heron, redshank, godwit, lapwing, sandpiper, shag, turnstone, swan, curlew, kingfisher, fulmar, oystercatcher, falcon, raven and perhaps the little egret or Cornish chough. Although having red legs and a long curved red bill, the Cornish chough is rather similar to the crow or jackdaw, being a rare yet very welcome sight along the cliffs.

Walking trips are a must here. Picnics are a fun way to walk and just think of all that healthy exercise. There are coastal and inland walks to enjoy, varying from the gentle to the very strenuous. The Hall Walk is very popular, as are walks along the cliffs beyond Polruan and St. Catherine's Castle and upstream around the various inlets of the River Fowey. It is well worth taking a pair of stout boots, a map, one of the excellent guidebooks on local walks and perhaps some waterproofs. Don't be too ambitious at first if not a seasoned rambler and remember to always follow the Country Code.

Along the way, Cornish flora and fauna is of great interest and again detailed guidebooks are useful, if only to identify clumps of valerian, known to 'Q' as the 'Pride of Fowey' and recognise the various types of lichen that thrive in the clean air. It is of interest to note that the roots of valerian can be used as a cure for hysteria and other such nervous conditions. It has a calming effect and perhaps is needed sometimes by the locals when dealing with tourists!

There is a tradition of authors in these parts, led by such notables as Sir Arthur Quiller-Couch, Daphne du Maurier, Leo Warmsley and Denys Val Baker. A much earlier satirical writer who once lived near The Ship Inn, at the premises now occupied by 'Julian Foye' was one John Wolcot, better known as 'Peter Pindar', who died in 1819. Roden Noel wrote the poem *Fowey* in the second half of the 19th century. The well-loved illustrator Mabel Lucie Atwell lived in Fowey for the last 20 years of her life in a house to the rear of the Fowey Hotel, until her death in 1964. There are also modern authors associated with Fowey such as Tim Heald and Sean Dorman.

SIR ARTHUR QUILLER-COUCH

Famous author Sir Arthur Quiller-Couch (1863-1944), often referred to by his pseudonym 'Q', was born in Bodmin in 1863. From 1892, he lived here in his beloved Fowey, which he referred to as 'Troy Town' in novels such as *The Mayor of Troy* and *The Astonishing History of Troy Town*. Fowey was also featured in some of his many other books, such as *Hocken and Hunkin* and *Shining Ferry*. The area around Fowey was even once known as 'Q' country, whereas nowadays it is often referred to as 'du Maurier' country. He was knighted in 1916.

'Q' lived above Whitehouse Quay, by the Polruan and Mevagissey ferry point slipway, in a house aptly named The Haven. Many authors and alike often visited, enjoying both his company and the splendid views. He called Cornwall the 'Delectable Duchy' and 'Q's heart and mind never strayed far from Fowey. He married a local girl, Louisa Hicks, in the local church, named his only daughter Foy and even became mayor here in 1937.

'Q' died in 1944 and was buried high above the town in Fowey Cemetery, Green Lane. It is tribute indeed to this great man that in 1948 a large granite memorial was erected in his memory overlooking the harbour along the Hall Walk, close to Bodinnick village.

Many of his personal books were bequeathed to the local library. Some of his work is still in print and there is a wealth of old 'Q' books available locally. To see his memorial and for the views alone, it is well worth a trip along the Hall Walk, even if not fully completed.

ALONG THE ESPLANADE

Readymoney Cove is but a short walk from the centre of Fowey, along the Esplanade. From the town quay, beyond the museum, walk a little way up the hill, through Trafalgar Square; bearing left past the Ship Inn public house and it is clearly signposted to the left, just past the old United Reform Church.

Along the Esplanade can be found a gate to the left that leads down to the small and quiet Grammar School Gardens. These are well stocked and the view from the memorial benches is breathtaking. Further along the road can be seen author Sir Arthur Quiller-Couch's old house 'The Haven' by Whitehouse Slip. There are public toilets here below the red shipping beacon and a children's paddling pool. Nearby is a shelter donated and dedicated to the people of Fowey from the thankful American Naval Advanced Amphibious Training Force, based here during the war in 1943. Below is Whitehouse Beach, compact and pleasant enough but which disappears at high tide.

Further along the Esplanade is the elegant Fowey Hotel, built in 1882, and a variety of other Victorian buildings. It is indeed a great delight to sit in the tea garden of the Fowey Hotel, formally the croquet lawn and partake

of a traditional Cornish cream tea, whilst admiring the panorama set out, it seems, solely for one's own personal delight.

The views across to Polruan are wonderful from the Esplanade and are made even more spectacular when viewed through the several holes in the wall of Crabpot Cottage. A ready framed picture if ever there was one.

READYMONEY COVE

This picturesque cove, guarded by an ancient castle to one side and an elegant stone house to the other, is very popular with beach-loving tourists. Be sure to check the tides as high tide means much less beach. There are no shops here, but an ice-cream van often is.

The name brings to mind thoughts of smugglers' treasure, caves and wreckers. In fact, rather unromantically, the name probably comes from 'redeman', meaning a 'ford of stones', although it is known that smuggling did occur in this area.

Daphne du Maurier lived here briefly from 1942 to 1943 and a blue commemorative plaque can be seen on one of the buildings, which is the former stables and coach house for the nearby grand house, Point Neptune. It is said that the sound of ghostly hooves can still be heard in these parts from time to time!

A grassed area with seating and small pointed turrets can be seen above the shore. This is the site of the old limekilns, which were originally built in 1819 and converted in 1935 when a public shelter was created beneath, along with public toilets.

POINT NEPTUNE HOUSE

Built in the 1860s this grand residence was constructed for William Rashleigh a few years before his death. Interestingly enough he is buried close to the nearby castle on the headland.

He preferred living here to residing in his family home at nearby Menabilly, which was where Daphne du Maurier later once lived, being 'Manderley' in her famous story *Rebecca*.

Point Neptune is a private residence and its solidly constructed yet intricate cast-iron gates are as impressive as the stone house itself. A grand old building indeed.

Opposite the gates is St. Catherine's Parade, a lovely lane that makes for a pleasant walk up through the woods to the main road. From there, turning right will lead back down into central Fowey. Bearing left, then left again and finally just before Coombe Farm turning left once more will lead back down into Readymoney Cove. Either head straight through Covington Wood or take the slightly longer route via part of the headland and Allday's Field, which was once part of Fowey Golf Club. Several of the old greens can easily be mistaken for archaeological features of great antiquity, which they are obviously not.

ST. CATHERINE'S CASTLE

From the beach the castle can be reached by ascending the steps in the corner (if high tides haven't washed them away again) and following the steep pathway to the top. For a slightly more gentle route up just follow the path round the back of the old cottages and bear left as the main track, charmingly named Love Lane bends to the right.

This atmospheric stronghold, now an English Heritage site, was constructed about 1540 forming part of Henry VIII's coastal defences. St. Catherine's Chapel previously stood on this headland. The castle was restored in 1855 and has at its base an interesting double gun platform. It was fortified again during the Second World War.

St. Catherine's Castle is a must to visit, as the breathtaking views are just totally stunning. Entry is free and it is open all year round.

Beyond the castle are beautiful walks along both the ancient trade routes of the 'Saints Way', towards Padstow (follow the Celtic cross signs) and also along the coastal path towards Polridmouth, the Gribben Head (with its 'Daymark' beacon built in 1832 by Trinity House), Polkerris and the Rashleigh Arms (follow the acorn signs).

RASHLEIGH MAUSOLEUM

Behind St. Catherine's Castle, obscured now by trees, is the resting place of William Rashleigh, his wife and daughter.

This grand mausoleum was built in 1866 and overlooks the family's beloved Fowey home, Point Neptune. It is of rather regal design and once looked out upon a clear and spectacular view of the harbour and also out to sea. Some of the family pets are buried near a lower pathway, even having their own small headstones. Sadly these rather touching graves have been smothered and lost beneath the ever-creeping undergrowth.

It was about here that St. Catherine's Chapel once stood, twin to the 13th century St. Saviour's Chapel, the ruins of which can be seen on the Polruan headland opposite. Both were places of religious worship and also helped sailors navigate into the safety of the harbour by means of bells and beacons of fire. Comfort indeed, in the middle of a tempest, to be shown the light, the redeeming way undeniably to be given shelter from the storm.

TOWARDS CAFFA MILL

From the Town Quay, beyond the main shops of Fore Street and the elegant Georgian building which houses the post office at Customs House Hill, heading towards the car ferry at Bodinnick, the buildings become more residential.

From the above route through the centre of Fowey, another via Bull Hill can be taken. The start of this is to be found by the Daphne du Maurier Literary Centre, close to the church. Here, to the right, a flight of steps lead up and the scenic narrow lane winds round the back of Fore Street, above the shop rooftops, ending back down at the start of North Street. Along here, as throughout Fowey, may be seen the very distinctive original street lamps, long since converted to electricity but still giving that very old fashioned feel to the place.

The exteriors of a great many buildings in Fowey have preservation orders on them, so that they will not be altered or spoilt in any way. Thus, the town's heritage cannot be modernised or lost to the whims of fashion.

Whichever way is taken, first North Street and then Passage Street wind their way down towards the car-ferry point at Caffa Mill. There are a few interesting shops and businesses along the way, including a pottery, a canoe and motorboat expedition centre, the Royal National Lifeboat Institute shop and more.

The route is narrow in places, often without the luxury of pavements, so beware of any traffic approaching from behind. Gaps in between the buildings often afford good views of the river and the wooded hillside opposite.

CAFFA MILL

The car park at Caffa Mill was built over the old wharves and inlet of Caffa Mill Pill. There are public toilets here as well as parking for boats, trailers and cars. It is advisable to park before purchasing a ticket, as spaces can often be hard to find and note that weekly passes are available at reduced rates. This also applies to the other local main car parks. There is a public slipway for launching small watercraft here. The car ferry journey over to Bodinnick, which accepts foot-passengers, is frequent, short and quick.

THIS OBELISK WAS FORMERLY ERECTED ON ALBERT QUAY TO MARK THE LANDING OF QUEEN VICTORIA AND PRINCE ALBERT THERE ON SEPTEMBER 8TH, 1846.

AS A SILVER JUBILEE TRIBUTE, AND TO COMMEMORATE THE VISIT OF HER MAJESTY QUEEN ELIZABETH II AND PRINCE PHILIP TO FOWEY IN 1962, IT WAS RECOVERED FROM THE HARBOUR BED WHERE IT HAD LAIN FOR MANY YEARS AND ERECTED ON THIS CAFFA MILL SITE. 1977.

In one corner can be seen part of an obelisk commemorating the visit to Fowey of Queen Victoria and Prince Albert, taking the appearance of an Egyptian needle. It was formally situated on Albert Quay in Fore Street, which was where the royal couple first landed in 1846, when it was known as Broad Slip.

Beyond the car park is the old Great Western Railway station, the private entrance to the IMERYS Minerals Ltd. china clay docks, the library and Station Wood. Before the demise of this railway line (which opened in 1860 and closed at the hand of Dr. Beeching in the 1960s) the route between Lostwithiel and Fowey was one of the country's most beautiful, affording magnificent views of the river. Nowadays, the nearest railway links are at Par and St. Austell although sadly not a steam train in sight. Modern electric and diesel trains, new fast roads and airports like Newquay have all helped to make access to Cornwall quick and easy.

Beyond the library, which is housed in the former customs house, is the beautiful Station Wood, accessed through a large dark gate (not the big white one). Here, following the path up to the right, an ancient rocking-stone, known as a Cornish 'logan-stone' can be seen. Natural weathering resulting in a large stone being left delicately balanced causes this interesting phenomenon. Although the stone no longer moves, the views further along the footpath are well worth the walk and will move you!

LOCAL GEOLOGY

Looking at the local cliffs and exposed outcrops it's difficult to comprehend their true age. In fact, the rocks around the Fowey area date from pre-Jurassic times, being over four hundred million (400,000,000) years old! They have been much affected by intense heat and belong to the Lower Devonian Meadfoot Beds that include siltstones, limestones and slates.

Nearby St. Austell is associated with the china clay industry and the granites of Bodmin Moor. It is the effect of hydrothermal processes (super hot, volatile, underground water solutions and gases) acting on granite that cause this valuable by-product. The mineral feldspar, within the granite, is decomposed and results in kaolin, which is the mineralogical name for china clay.

CHINA CLAY DOCKS

The china clay docks at Fowey are to be found a little upstream from the car ferry. Here they export vast quantities annually which are used in such industries as ceramics and paper. Large ships are constantly visiting the jetties aided by the pilots and tugboats. They enter the harbour empty, leaving fully laden on the high tide bound for destinations all over the world. Upstream beyond the docks are Golant, Lerryn, St. Winnow and Lostwithiel. All are worth visiting and boat trips are available if tidal conditions are favourable.

A little past the docks are situated the 'Old Sawmills', now a recording studio but once the base of the United States Army 'Advanced Amphibious Training Force' during the Second World War, when they were preparing for D-Day. In the 1960s and early 1970s this was the home of author Denys Val Baker, who wrote about his life here in books such as *Life up the Creek* and *An Old Mill by the Stream*.

BODINNICK

This quaint, compact village, whose name means fortified dwelling, is focused around the ferry point. Access to the highly scenic Hall Walk can be gained halfway up the hill, a little way past the small church of St. John the Baptist, both on the right hand side. Look out for the sign stating 'Hall Walk Polruan 4 miles' as it can easily be missed.

The Old Ferry Inn is of historic interest being around 400 years old and the interior is fascinating. Outside it has two distinctive signs (one a wonderful painting of the old 'horse' ferry) and great views back down to the ferry and over to Fowey.

FERRYSIDE

This impressive dwelling was formally used for boat building. It lies right at the water's edge next to the Bodinnick ferry slipway and is aptly named 'Ferryside', a former home of author Daphne du Maurier (1907-1989). Here she found 'personal freedom' and wrote her first novel *The Loving Spirit*, which was based upon the Slade family of Polruan. The figurehead of the schooner *Jane Slade* can be seen on the right hand side of the building, just below her old bedroom. It was rescued from the mud of Pont Pill where the rotting ship lay abandoned.

In 1942 Daphne du Maurier leased a former stable block at Readymoney Cove, Fowey. A year later she left and leased nearby Menabilly House, the country mansion of the Rashleigh family and her 'house of secrets'. This home became 'Manderley' in the story *Rebecca* and she also set *The King's General* and *My Cousin Rachel* there. She became Dame Daphne du Maurier in 1969 and in the same year moved yet again, this time to Kilmarth, close to nearby Polkerris. There she felt 'at one with the house', which became *The House on the Strand*. Daphne also wrote *The Birds*, *Frenchman's Creek* and *Rule Britannia* there. When she died in 1989, her ashes were scattered above the local Cornish cliffs she grew to love so dearly.

There is the 'Daphne Du Maurier Literary Centre' to visit, located next to the church near the Town Quay in Fowey. Guided walks and talks are available and an annual festival is held in May. Many of her books are on sale locally.

Ferryside is still a private dwelling, currently the residence of Daphne's son Christian du Maurier Browning. It seems fitting somehow that Ferryside is still in the ownership of the family after all these years and remains much as it did when first purchased back in 1926.

PRIME CELLARS

A little further along the waterline, downstream from Ferryside and towards Pont Pill, can be found Prime Cellars. This isolated and most interesting building is an enchanting landmark. It has massive doors, a quaint buckled roof and has recently undergone complete sensitive renovation.

Gazing over at this rather lonely building it is hard to imagine it being much more than a fisherman's riverside cottage. However, in its long and varied past it has been such things as a boathouse to the manor of Hall, a private dwelling known as 'Prime House' as recorded in a painting of 1769 when a Mary Elliot lived here, a pilchard cellar, a coal and wood store, a boat shed and a workshop. There is talk of it even being used as a radio communications centre during World War Two. It was apparently also an inn, an alehouse, supplying customers who had to arrive and depart by water, due to the isolated position. A tricky manoeuvre even when sober!

This building and in particular, its steep, now overgrown garden, has been visited by some famous literary geniuses. Kenneth Grahame of *Wind in the Willows* fame, J.M. Barrie of *Peter Pan* fame; A.L.Rowse, foremost Cornish writer of his day and Daphne du Maurier among others. They have all been here as guests of Sir Arthur Quiller-Couch, who held the tenancy. They would be rowed over in 'Q's small boat. He cultivated the steep land behind, naming it 'The Farm', although it is unlikely that 'Q' kept any livestock here. He did, however, write a short story about it, called *Priam's Cellars*.

HALL WALK

This is considered one of the best Cornish walks in one of the UK's most popular places to live. Little wonder really, as it boasts both stunning harbour and countryside views. The walk is yet another step into Fowey's rich, historic past and is well worth the time it takes to complete.

Stretching from Bodinnick via Pont to Polruan, its near four-mile beautiful route along protected National Trust land is a must for both visitors and locals alike. There are many benches along the way for that well-earned rest. The beauty of the trees and the variety of wild flowers are a delight whatever the season.

It was named the 'Hall' walk after a once nearby manor house of Hall and was part of its Elizabethan promenade. The house was the residence of the Mohun family but was sadly destroyed during the Civil War of the 17th century. The chapel now renovated still survives.

It is also sometimes called the King's Walk, as King Charles I was almost murdered here in 1644, during the Civil War. The story is told on a plaque in the ancient shelter or summerhouse building close to 'Q's memorial at the top of Penleath Point, in his daughter's own words.

This incident occurred only a few years before Charles was beheaded in 1649 and ironically there is a wooden board in Fowey church, which is by way of a letter of thanks from the king to the loyal people of Cornwall, dated 1643. The large granite memorial stone here was erected to the memory of author Sir Arthur Quiller-Couch in 1948. It dominates the headland and spectacular harbour views are to be enjoyed from this vantage point.

To avoid any confusion, it is worth noting that there are two different memorial stones to be found near the Bodinnick end of the walk. Both have references to 'Q', the above-mentioned and also a smaller war memorial.

TO THE MEMORY OF
SIR ARTHUR T. QUILLER-COUCH
GREAT CORNISHMAN : WRITER : SCHOLAR
BORN AT BODMIN 1863 : DIED AT FOWEY 1944
BY HIS GENIUS AS AN AUTHOR AND AS AN EDITOR
HE ENRICHED THE LITERATURE OF ENGLAND
AND BROUGHT HONOUR TO HIS COUNTY AND
TO FOWEY, HIS HOME FOR OVER FIFTY YEARS.

HON. FELLOW OF TRINITY COLLEGE OXFORD AND
OF JESUS COLLEGE CAMBRIDGE. KING EDWARD VII
PROFESSOR OF ENGLISH LITERATURE AT CAMBRIDGE
HE WAS EMINENT ALIKE IN LEARNING AND IN
HIS LONG SERVICE TO BOTH UNIVERSITIES
AND TO EDUCATION IN CORNWALL

COURTEOUS IN MANNER, CHARITABLE IN
JUDGEMENT, CHIVALROUS IN ACTION; HE
MANIFESTED IN LIFE AS IN LITERATURE
THE DIGNITY OF MANHOOD, THE SANCTITY
OF HOME AND THE SOVEREIGNTY OF GOD.

From Penleath Point and the 'Q' memorial the walk follows round Pont Pill creek, crossing down over at Pont footbridge where there is an interesting old notice board, dated 1894.

From here the footpath continues right round into central Polruan: look out for the 'money' tree on the way. The ferry back to Fowey may be taken at the town quay. The whole walk can just as easily be enjoyed in reverse, namely from Polruan to Bodinnick.

PONT PILL

Pont Pill, which means 'bridge creek', is also known as Pont Creek. It was here that Daphne du Maurier gained inspiration for her first novel. She also travelled along this inlet by boat on her wedding day in 1932 to be married at St. Wyllow's church Lanteglos, to Major 'Tommy' Browning.

They honeymooned at Frenchman's Creek, near Helford, and this later became the title of a story Daphne wrote about the love of a French pirate. Although not really set at Pont Pill, it is easy to imagine that it was when reading the story.

Kenneth Grahame, who was married in Fowey in 1899, often went for boat trips around here with 'Q' and friends. The local scenery surely inspired his work and he even refers to Fowey in his classic children's story *Wind in the Willows* as 'the little grey sea town that clings along one steep side of the harbour.'

I wonder if Toad Hall was modelled on Fowey Hall and if the Sea Rat had his origins here?

In a letter of 1899, Kenneth Grahame writing from Fowey stated that his sister had gone along the cliffs locally and climbed down to a little cove. As she sat there, a big rat came out and sitting beside her, began eating winkles. This is presumably the beginning of the Sea Rat character 'the wayfarer', to be found in the 'Wayfarers All' chapter of *Wind in the Willows*, first published in 1908. The Sea Rat even mentions shellfish, the pleasant harbours of Cornwall and the little grey sea town quote. The story is well worth reading again, especially whilst out and about locally.

Author Leo Warmsley lived along Pont Pill in the early 1960s writing about his time in the area and this resulted in such books as *Paradise Creek a*nd *Love in the Sun*.

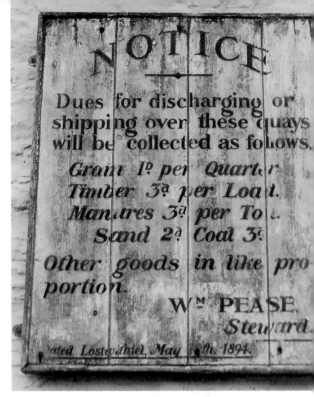

POLRUAN

Hugging the steep hillside on the opposite side to Fowey, Polruan is a typically picturesque old fishing and shipbuilding village, which seems to have lost little of its character over the years. It is picture postcard perfect. The name is possibly derived from 'pol' meaning pool and 'ruan' meaning river, so Polruan is the 'pool by the river' or it may mean the 'cove of Ruan'.

It is steeped in history, sadly has very few shops now and possesses steep hills. A couple of small beaches are exposed when the tide is low. There is much to explore but just to relax over a coffee, maybe a drink in an inn, or by the town quay just watching the world go by, is a totally enjoyable way of passing the time. In Daphne du Maurier's first novel *The Loving Spirit*, Polruan is referred to as 'Plyn' and is the setting for the story. Holly House, the real 'Ivy House', can be found in Fore Street a little way up the main hill on the right hand side. To come to this quaint old village and sit reading her work brings characters and places to life. It transports Polruan back in time, especially if the boat yards are busy at work.

Some of the houses here show a typical Cornish feature, a very long staircase window, which helps to let in more light.

The quayside, headland, Blockhouse and surrounding area are all well worth exploring and the passenger ferry from Fowey makes Polruan easily accessible. The walk along the coast path to Lantic Bay, Lantivet Bay and beyond to Polperro affords stunning views. On a clear day, the Eddistone Lighthouse, nearly 20 miles away, can be seen.

To access the Hall Walk from Polruan, proceed along Chapel Lane above the boatyards and follow the signs to Hall Walk.

Polruan boasts two old character public houses both situated close to the town quay. The Lugger is very close to the ferry point and inside it, a very apt sign for these parts reads 'a boat is a hole in the water surrounded by wood and into which one pours money'! The Russell Inn, once run by the Slade family, can be reached by a flight of steps between the houses at the end of the Lugger, or also via Fore Street and then West Street. The public toilets are located by the ferry point on the town quay and also higher up at St. Saviour's car park.

During World War Two, a daylight raid by a German bomber demolished Polruan School, now the site of the car park, but luckily there were no fatalities. In fact, both here and in Fowey, war damage was kept to a thankful minimum. One of the large gardens, 'Headland', is open to the public at certain times helping to boost lifeboat funds. It is situated in Battery Lane not far from the Blockhouse.

At the top of the headland the ruins of St.Saviour's 13th century chapel stand guard over the community. A similar chapel, St. Catherine's, once stood on the Fowey headland opposite. Both were used not just for religious purposes, but also as shipping aids to help sailors navigate through the perilous jaws of the harbour.

BLOCKHOUSE

This substantial square building is variously referred to as the Blockhouse, Blocking Castle, Polruan Castle, or just the Castle. It was built about 1380 after an attack by the Spanish and the inaccessible ruins of its twin lie opposite on the Fowey side of the river.

A mighty chain was once strung between the two thus protecting the harbour from ancient attack. The grooves this made in the rocks below the Polruan Blockhouse can still be seen. An anti-submarine net apparently served the same sort of purpose during World War Two.

The Blockhouse is a favoured spot for fishermen and a prime vantage point for fine views out to sea, over to Fowey and of the harbour. At this spot it is easy to imagine cannon balls flying as Spanish ships attacked. These projectiles are sometimes found in and around the harbour.

BEYOND FOWEY

There is much to see in Fowey; in fact one can easily spend an entire holiday just within its bounds. However, beyond Fowey a lot more is to be seen and enjoyed.

Nearby are the coastal villages of Polperro, Looe, Charlestown, and Mevagissey, all having special charms of their own. Inland are such places to visit as the famous Eden Project near St. Austell as well as St.Austell itself, Castle Dore, Restormel Castle, Lostwithiel, Golitha Falls, Bodmin Moor, Lanhydrock House, Luxulyan Valley, Launceston and the Lost Gardens of Heligan, to name but a few.

Further afield are centres such as Truro, Redruth, Falmouth, Helston and Penzance to enjoy in Cornwall and Plymouth just over the border in Devon. There are many smaller places all well worth seeking out.

About two miles out on the road towards Par and St. Austell, on the very outskirts of Fowey, a rather interesting and ancient stone can be seen. This is known as Tristan's Stone and was carved in the 6th century. It is thought to have links with the tragic love story between Tristan, son of King Mark of Cornwall and Iseult.

A nearby information plaque placed there by the Fowey Old Cornwall Society tells the story. This 'longstone' originally stood, not in Fowey, but close to Castle Dore, a nearby ancient Iron Age hill fort, thought to be the site of King Mark's palace.

Standing by this lichen-covered relic one feels somehow in touch with the past and so connected to the story. This is re-told in the book *Castle Dor*, the manuscript of which was left unfinished by Sir Arthur Quiller-Couch upon his death in 1944. Daphne du Maurier was subsequently asked to complete this and the resulting story is still in print.